Praise for *The Gospel according to* The Simpsons™ *The Spiritual Life of the World's Most Animated Family*

"Religion journalist Pinsky offers a thoughtful and genuinely entertaining review of faith and morality as reflected through the irreverently sweet comedy of *The Simpsons*, drawing on a wide if not encyclopedic knowledge of key episodes and interviews with the series' creators. Pinsky reminds readers that ultimately the abiding charm of the show is how often its caricatures are devastatingly on-target and point to a deeper truth."
  —*Publishers Weekly*

"On the heels of *The Simpsons and Philosophy* comes a seriously funny examination of the spirituality of the popular TV show. . . . Pinsky makes a compelling argument that the show's writers' view of religious expression is complicated and sympathetic."
  —*Booklist*

"A straight-faced (yet unavoidably amusing) look at the program's treatment of faith, ethics and, yes, 'family values.'"
  —*Toronto Star*

"*The Simpsons* is one of the most subtle pieces of propaganda around in the cause of sense, humility and virtue. Mark Pinsky manages to decipher the code without deadening the humour, which is quite an achievement."
  —The Most Rev. Dr. Rowan Williams, Archbishop of Wales

"What a fun book—with serious purpose. Pinsky has taken a pop culture icon and, through the eyes of faith, made an incisive and loving critique of our culture. I didn't know that Bart Simpson had so much to teach us. Far out!"
  —Will Willimon, Dean of the Chapel, Duke University

D0017494

The Gospel according to
The Simpsons™

The Gospel according to
The Simpsons™

Leader's Guide for Group Study

Mark I. Pinsky
and Samuel F. (Skip) Parvin

Westminster John Knox Press
LOUISVILLE • LONDON

Scripture quotations from the New Revised Standard Version of the Bible are copyright © 1989 by the Division of Christian Education of the National Council of the Churches of Christ in the U.S.A., and are used by permission.

Book design by Sharon Adams
Cover illustrated by Teri Vinson

First edition
Published by Westminster John Knox Press
Louisville, Kentucky

This book is printed on acid-free paper that meets the American National Standards Institute Z39.48 standard. ∞

PRINTED IN THE UNITED STATES OF AMERICA

02 03 04 05 06 07 08 09 10 11 — 10 9 8 7 6 5 4 3 2

Library of Congress Cataloging-in-Publication Data

Pinsky, Mark I., 1947–
   The Gospel according to the Simpsons : leaders guide for group study / Mark I. Pinsky and Samuel Parvin.— 1st ed.
      p. cm.
   ISBN 0-664-22590-X (alk. paper)
   1. Simpsons (Television program) 2. Television broadcasting—Religious aspects. I. Parvin, Samuel F., 1953– II. Title.

PN1992.77.S58 P55 2002
791.45'72—dc21

                                                      200216854

Contents

Introduction

I am a committed Jew, despite the earnest ministrations of legions of well-meaning, evangelical Christians. So I might not be the first person you think of to design a Sunday school curriculum guide—even one based on a book that I wrote. Nonetheless, as a religion writer in the heart of the American Sunbelt, I think I probably spend more time in church each month than lots of Christians. And one thing I have learned for certain from this reporting is how important religious leaders—clergy and lay—believe it is to communicate the importance of faith and belief to teens and young adults. A consensus seems to be forming in this country that popular culture may be one avenue to reach people not otherwise inclined to church, if only by stealth. Maybe it's because I write a lot about the intersection of religion and popular culture, but I seem to see evidence of this trend everywhere.

Consider: On a Sunday night in December 2001, a cartoon character in a popular prime-time television sitcom, distraught over changes at the Protestant church where her family worships every week, decides to convert to Buddhism. The episode was appropriately titled "She of Little Faith." At the same time this episode of *The Simpsons* aired, on another network, *Touched by an Angel* dramatized the story of a woman who lost a friend in the September 11 terrorist attacks. Paralyzed with fear and anxiety, the woman is visited by an angel who assures her that God will be with her always. A week later—by popular demand—an episode of the comedy-drama *Ally McBeal* was repeated in which the title character tries to comfort a minister whose faith is shaken by his wife's murder. Don't be shocked. These episodes are not an aberration for commercial television, long considered the devil's playground. Little by little, Hollywood writers and producers are discovering that faith may actually have some entertainment value.

For decades—and for a number of complex reasons, mostly involving fear of offending—prime-time programming has consistently avoided religion. This despite the fact that, according to pollsters from George Gallup to George Barna, faith forms such a large part of the lives of most Americans on the other side of the screen.

"It *is* something new, because religion is the last frontier that commercial television was willing to foray into," says Robert Thompson, professor of media and popular culture at Syracuse University. "Religion was the one place that they pretty much steered clear of. Popular culture was supposed to comfort people. Religion, the idea went, made people uncomfortable. Television executives felt that if they reflected the real world in prime-time entertainment, then people would reject it. They really believed that entertainment was an anesthesia to what was going on in the news."

Of course, not all academics agree. "Religion comes and goes on prime time, depending on Hollywood folklore about what attracts audiences," says Quentin Schultze, professor of communication at Calvin College, an evangelical Christian school in Grand Rapids, Michigan. "When the economy goes into a tailspin or something horrendous happens in the news—like the September 11 disasters—television and film writers sense that spirituality is important to people."

In recent television seasons, this cyclical role of religion on television has begun to change, perhaps fundamentally, with the ratings success (or at least survival) of shows built around religion and spirituality, such as *Touched By an Angel* and *7th Heaven*. Viewers have signaled their willingness to accept a devout bailiff in *Judging Amy*, a goofy but believing brother on *Maybe It's Me*, and a praying (if argumentative) president in *The West Wing*. Even on the scatological *South Park*, Jesus wrestles with Satan—winning only because the Prince of Darkness bets against himself and throws the fight.

"What entertainment producers have figured out, and what some religious leaders are still struggling to comprehend, is that this religion is increasingly pluralistic and less tied to creed and dogma," says Teresa Blythe, coauthor of *Watching What We Watch: Prime-Time Television through the Lens of Faith*. "That's why we see story lines involving a lot of different religions. As it became fashionable to portray Buddhist or New Age spirituality, it became more acceptable to portray all varieties of Christian spirituality."

What is going on here? This is a long way from *M*A*S*H*'s ineffectual Catholic chaplain, Father Mulcahy. Should Bill Moyers be concerned that the commercial networks are encroaching on his PBS turf? "Hardly," says Blythe. "Commercial networks exist for one reason—to make money. They will most likely use religion in story lines or documentaries only to the point that it helps sell advertising time. As soon as religion starts stepping on toes and demanding economic justice for all, television will pull back." Schultze agrees, to an extent, but he sees other problems. "There's more than enough room for gaggles of religious characters and plots on mainstream television," he says. "The problem is not whether audiences are interested in spiritual matters, but rather the fact that so many writers and producers don't have religious experiences to call upon. Hollywood is not the most devout place on the planet."

There is little debate over the value and power of popular culture in providing moral, if not religious, instruction for young children. Think about the messages and lessons about good always being rewarded and evil always punished that are presented in Walt Disney's animated features, such as *Snow White* and *Pinocchio*. More recently, Disney's *Lion King* video, with its "great circle of life" philosophy, sold tens of millions of copies after having made hundreds of millions of dollars at the box office. DreamWorks's *Prince of Egypt*, the story of Moses and the exodus, was hailed by religious leaders across the theological spectrum, many of whom were consulted on the production of the animated feature.

And the cartoon images don't have to move to deliver their message. Comic strip writers are no longer hesitant to draw on the divine. Although pioneered by Charles Schulz in *Peanuts*, religious references are now as likely to show up in modern strips such as *Rose Is Rose* and *Wildwood* as they are in more venerable strips such as *Dennis the Menace*, *B.C.*, *Beetle Bailey*, and *Family Circus*. "Comedy and faith are natural partners in storytelling," says Calvin's Professor Schultze. "Comedy shows us how silly we are, the crazy situations we get ourselves into even when we are trying to be good. Just as television is the nation's jester, the daily comics are our one-minute homilies. The comics are about our foolishness—even how we survive with grace."

Clearly something is at work, because the growing traffic between religion and popular culture seems to be traveling in both directions. In increasing numbers, American religious leaders are turning to popular culture to communicate their theological values. "Television and film producers are the modern-day storytellers who have to stay in touch with what viewers believe is important, which includes religion. They don't always get it right, but the fact that they have noticed that viewers can not only take religious subject matter but actually enjoy it, has energized some religious leaders in this country—at least those willing to recognize that popular culture matters," says Blythe. Christian study Bibles and Sunday school curricula—such as the one you are about to read—have already been developed based on such 1960s and 1970s television staples as *The Andy Griffith Show*, *The Beverly Hillbillies*, and *The Brady Bunch*. Syracuse's Thompson, himself a former Sunday school teacher at his Presbyterian church, sees nothing wrong with this trend, calling it "entry-level religion" that serves a good purpose.

There are countless more examples: The Evangelical Lutheran Church in America hopes to resurrect its beloved stop-action animated children's show, *Davey and Goliath*; a respected rabbi in Orlando teaches a well-attended course on *"Star Trek* and Judaism"; FM radio stations across the nation have adopted the "Contemporary Christian Music" format, making them sound—except for the songs' evangelical lyrics—like any other rock station; and there are more than forty-five million copies in print of Jerry Jenkins's and Tim LaHaye's *Left Behind* series of potboiler novels based on the book of Revelation (with a new LaHaye series coming about a Christian archaeologist who sounds a lot like the big screen hero Indiana Jones). VeggieTales have sold twenty-five million videos and three million music CDs, with a full-length feature film coming next.

In fact, there appears to be no limit to this trend of appropriating and adapting popular culture in the service of religion, particularly for those who prefer their theology literal, "lite," and concrete. An evangelical group in Orlando hired a top-of-the line theme park designer to develop "The Holy Land Experience," a small, Bible-based tourist attraction near Universal Studios. Costumed characters, including Jesus (in season) roam a small recreation of first-century Jerusalem. The park, which describes itself as a "living Bible museum," claims its goal is to provide "a wholesome, family-oriented, educational and entertainment facility, where people can come and be encouraged, instructed and reinforced in their faith."

Is all this a good thing? Frankly, I'm of two minds on the intermingling of faith and entertainment. On the one hand, resorting to such lowest-common-denominator vehicles has the aroma of desperation on the part of organized religion. It is further evidence—if any more is needed—of the evaporating attention span of most Americans, and of the general dumbing down of serious discourse. Yet, undeniably, popular culture appears successful as a reference point in drawing in, on its level, many of the "unchurched," which accounts for my preparing this guide and for your reading it.

The debate over utilizing popular culture for evangelical purposes has been going on for a long time. During the Protestant

Reformation five hundred years ago, Martin Luther was attacked for cribbing tavern ballad melodies for hymns. He is said to have retorted, "Why should the devil have all the good songs?" Terrence Lindvall, professor of communication at Pat Robertson's Regent University in Virginia Beach, thinks this debate will continue. "The pendulum of faith in culture and faith opposing culture will continue to swing," he said. "At present, the parables and icons of the faith are colorfully animated for the entertainment of the churched and unchurched. Doctrine and dogma are viewed with suspicion—although *The Simpsons* and even Disney are not without their invisible worldviews, doctrines, and ethics. All media recommend how people should live, some even intentionally. They advise how we should view our families, work, sex, and now, some are even promoting how we should understand religion. At the least, they will make it all entertaining."

Since I have always believed in truth in packaging, I need to tell you that most of the heavy lifting for this study guide was done by my coauthor, the Reverend Skip Parvin, pastor of Tuskawilla United Methodist Church, just outside Orlando. Skip has extensive experience in church youth work, writing, and analyzing popular culture from a religious and moral perspective. He knows what he is doing, which is why our editor at Westminster John Knox Press, David Dobson, chose him. This study guide is, to be sure, based on my book, *The Gospel according to* The Simpsons: *The Spiritual Life of the World's Most Animated Family*, and on an outline that I prepared. In addition, Skip and I consulted throughout the writing process. We have done our best to make this curriculum accessible to all religious groups and denominations. Scripture quotations are from both the Hebrew Bible and the New Testament. It goes without saying that *The Simpsons* episodes we have chosen can be appreciated by everyone, and I hope they will be.

How to Use This Guide

Each chapter of this study guide is centered around one episode of *The Simpsons* and is designed to stand alone as an individual session. Viewing the episode will require about thirty minutes, and we have provided enough in the way of activities and discussion questions to fill at least an additional hour. While each session has been created with youth and young adults in mind, we feel that the sessions can be converted easily to work well with adults. The setting for using these sessions is left up to the leader, and there are several options. The leader can use them for a youth group program, a Sunday school class, a Bible study, or in any other educational setting. The sessions can be used wherever a television and VCR are available. Despite the fact that each chapter is designed to stand alone, several of the sessions can be used in combination to form a *Simpsons* retreat or lock-in.

Always preview the episode you will be using at home before leading a session. Don't ever assume that you can remember everything about any episode. You will be surprised how much you can forget. The majority of these sessions are based on *Simpsons* episodes that are commercially available at your local video store or media outlet. (The name of the compilation tape that a particular episode can be found on is located in parentheses after the name of that episode in each chapter.) Many video rental stores carry *The Simpsons* collection as well. In most areas of the

United States, and in many countries around the world, *Simpsons* episodes are shown several times a day, which makes it convenient to watch an episode without having to purchase or rent it. Just contact your local Fox television affiliate and they will be happy to inform you when certain episodes will air. You can then schedule a time for your group to meet and watch the episode together.

This guide is designed to accompany the book *The Gospel according to* The Simpsons: *The Spiritual Life of the World's Most Animated Family* by Mark I. Pinsky. Though it is not necessary, it will be helpful if each participant has a copy of that book. You as leader will certainly want to have a copy. The book can be found in your local bookstore, and on the web at www.wjkbooks.com, or call 1-800-227-2872 to place an order or inquire about quantity discounts.

Note: Be aware of the warning at the beginning of videotapes or DVDs that you rent or purchase. The rental or purchase of home videocassettes or DVDs gives you the right to show them in a home setting only, unless you purchase a license to show them elsewhere. Check with your pastor or director of education to see if your church or school already has such a license.

Note for readers in Great Britain: Readers in Great Britain and Europe can also buy the book through their local bookstore, or they can contact the WJK office in London by phone at 020-8861-5871 or via e-mail at wjkuk@globalnet.co.uk.

Most of the episodes discussed in this guide are also available in Great Britain; however, the names of the tapes are different. Here is the list of the names of the tapes commercially available in Great Britain:

> Chapter 1: The Last Temptation of Homer, or The Simpsons: Year 2, Part 1
> Chapter 2: The Simpsons Greatest Hits
> Chapter 3: Not available in Great Britain

Chapter 4: Not available in Great Britain
Chapter 5: Heaven and Hell
Chapter 6: The Simpsons: Year 2, Box 2
Chapter 7: The Simpsons: Season 1
Chapter 8: The Simpsons: Year 2, Part 2
Chapter 9: Not available in Great Britain
Chapter 10: Heaven and Hell

One

What Is Important in Life?

Episode: "One Fish, Two Fish, Blowfish, Blue Fish"
(*The Best of* The Simpsons, vol. 7)

Synopsis: The Simpsons decide to go out to dinner to a new sushi restaurant. After sampling every other offering on the menu, Homer orders the blowfish, which, if not cut perfectly, can be poisonous. An apprentice sushi chef believes he has cut the fish incorrectly, and Homer is sent to the hospital where his doctor informs him that if he has ingested the poison, he has twenty-four hours to live. Homer, believing that he is going to die, makes a "to do" list of important things to accomplish in his last twenty-four hours on earth.

Supplementary Reading: Chapter 1 of *The Gospel according to* The Simpsons

Old Testament Scripture Lesson (Eccl. 3:1–8): For everything there is a season, and a time for every matter under heaven: a time to be born, and a time to die; a time to plant, and a time to pluck up what is planted; a time to kill, and a time to heal; a time to break down, and a time to build up; a time to weep, and a time to laugh; a time to mourn, and a time to dance; a time to throw away stones, and a time to gather stones together; a time to embrace, and a time to refrain from embracing; a time to seek, and a time to lose; a time to keep, and a time to throw away; a time to tear, and a time to sew; a time to keep silence, and a time to speak; a time to love, and a time to hate; a time for war, and a time for peace.

New Testament Scripture Lesson (Luke 12:16–21): Then he told them a parable: "The land of a rich man produced abundantly. And he thought to himself, 'What should I do, for I have no place to store my crops?' Then he said, 'I will do this: I will pull down my barns and build larger ones, and there I will store all my grain and my goods. And I will say to my soul, 'Soul, you have ample goods laid up for many years; relax, eat, drink, be merry.' But God said to him, 'You fool! This very night your life is being demanded of you. And the things you have prepared, whose will they be?' So it is with those who store up treasures for themselves but are not rich toward God."

Homer's List

1. Make list.
2. Eat a hearty breakfast.
3. Make videotape for Maggie.
4. Have man-to-man with Bart.
5. Listen to Lisa play her sax.
6. Make funeral arrangement.
7. Make peace with Dad.
8. Beer with the boys at the bar.
9. Tell off boss.
10. Go hang gliding.
11. Plant a tree.
12. A final dinner with my beloved family.

   And he adds, "Be intimate with Marge."

Activity: If I Died Tomorrow

Have group members each make a list of twelve things they would want to do if they knew they only had twenty-four hours to live. Ask them to take their lists seriously so that they will reflect the most important aspects of their lives. When they have finished, have volunteers share some of the items on their lists and discuss what the lists have to say about the priorities in their lives.

Questions for Discussion: Prior to the discussion, have a member of the group read aloud each of the Scripture lessons.

- Read Homer's list to the group and then ask participants how they feel about Homer's priorities.

- Compare Homer's list to yours. How does it differ? How is it similar?

- How do your priorities differ from Homer's? How are they similar?

- At the hospital, Homer is told by his doctor that if he has ingested the poison he will die in twenty-four hours. Following this revelation there is a humorous sequence in which the doctor gives Homer a pamphlet entitled "So You're Going to Die" and informs Homer about the five stages one experiences during the process of dying—denial, anger, fear, bargaining, and acceptance. Homer runs through all five steps as the doctor recites them. Discuss the stages in the dying process. Have you ever had experience with any of these stages, or have you seen them manifested in others?

- Marge suggests that they add "Watch the sunrise" to Homer's list. Marge then allows Homer to oversleep on "his last day on earth." Why does she do this? (She says Homer "looked so peaceful" sleeping. As always, Marge wants what seems to be best for her husband even if it means a few hours less to accomplish the tasks he has laid out for himself.)

- One of the items on Homer's list is to have a "man-to-man" with Bart. At first, Bart misunderstands and thinks Homer wants to punish him or chew him out. What does this say about Homer's relationship with his son? (Bart is used to relating to Homer in negative ways and is mystified by his father's attempt at positive interaction.)

- Part of the "wisdom" that Homer shares with Bart is "the three little sentences that will get you through life: 1. Cover for me. 2. Oh, good idea, boss. 3. It was like that when I got here." What does this have to say about who Homer is and what his priorities are? (Homer is a simple man who believes the cliché

"You have to go along to get along." He believes that what he is teaching Bart will make his life easier.)

- How does Bart respond to the man-to-man with Homer? (He calls it "good stuff." Later, when Homer is teaching Bart to shave, Bart knocks over the aftershave and breaks the bottle. When Homer starts to get angry, Bart immediately responds, "It was like that when I got here!" Homer sees this as evidence that Bart has taken his advice to heart.)

- When people are dying, they need to deal with their own personal grief. We don't anticipate Homer having that kind of depth of feeling. How does Homer deal with his personal grief? (There are many touching moments in which Homer expresses his personal grief. When he listens to the sad refrain that Lisa plays on her sax, he bursts into tears. When he is making Maggie's video, he tells her to remember him as "a simple, kind, gentle man who loved his children." When he goes to Moe's bar for a last beer with the boys, he confesses to them, "Sometimes when I'm at work I think of you and smile," and then kisses them goodbye. He tells his father how much he loves him. He is moved by Marge's poem. He says a fond farewell to his sleeping children.)

- When Homer goes next door to borrow the Flanderses' video camera to make Maggie's video, Ned invites him to a barbecue the next day. What does Homer's response have to say about him and his priorities? (As usual, Homer doesn't want to have anything to do with the Flanders family. Homer's humanity gets the best of him when he realizes that he can promise to be there and then not be available because he is dead. He decides to lie to Ned and even promises to bring some steaks, using the fact that he is dying to realize selfish purposes.)

- Homer goes to the nursing home to "make peace" with his father. What does Homer's visit with his father have to say about his priorities? (Once he's with his father, Homer laments that they never "went fishing, played catch, or hugged each other." He tells his father he loves him and then starts to leave, but his father calls him back with an invitation to go fishing. Homer agrees to spend the time with his dad and even crosses off some of the other priorities on his list to make more time for his dad. Of course, at one point, in typical Homer fashion, he says, "Gee, Dad, way to hog my last moments.")

- Do you think many people in this situation would place a high priority on "making peace" with their parents? Are problems with parents a universal concern?

- Do you think it odd that Homer, who considers himself a Christian, never talks about resurrection or at least about heaven?

- One of the last things Homer does is listen to "The Good Book" (the Bible) on tape, as narrated by Larry King. Do you think Homer is sincere in his desire to encounter the Scripture before he dies, or is this just another cliché? (Homer listens to the tape but quickly gets bored, fast-forwarding through the "begats." He seems to have a sincere desire to listen to "The Good Book" but, as usual, doesn't have the discipline to follow through and eventually falls asleep while listening.)

- The Larry King version of "The Good Book" ends with the verse: "And he shall turn the heart of the fathers to the children and the heart of the children to the fathers, lest I come and smite thee from the earth." What does this fabricated Bible verse have to say about the events of the day? (Actually, it foreshadows Homer's survival. During Homer's "last twenty-four hours," the hearts of the fathers have been turned to the children and the children to the fathers. It's almost as if God has chosen not to "smite" Homer from the earth.)

- When Marge discovers that Homer is alive, they begin to celebrate, and Homer vows "from this day forward to live life at its fullest." Do you think he will follow through on his promise? (The episode ends by cutting to a shot of Homer sitting on the couch eating pork rinds and watching bowling. The group can draw its own conclusions.)

Prayer: God our Creator, help us to value each moment of every day. We realize that there are no guarantees in this life and that any day could be our last. Guide us as we sort through our priorities so that we understand what is truly important. Help us to always place you first on our list. Amen.

Something to Talk About: This week find time to talk to someone you respect about the priorities in his or her life and how those priorities have been shaped by his or her faith.

Two

The Power of Prayer

Episode: "Bart Gets an F"
(*The Best of* The Simpsons, vol. 4)

S **ynopsis:** When Bart is called upon in class to give a book report on *Treasure Island,* he fails because he hasn't read the book. He also fails a history test and is told by the school psychologist that if he doesn't pass his next test, he'll be held back in the fourth grade for another year. The night before the test he realizes that he is not quite ready, so he prays that God will create a reason for school to close the next day so he will have one more day to study. During the night it snows, and when Bart wakes up he finds that the school has been closed.

Supplementary Reading: Chapter 2 of *The Gospel according to* The Simpsons

Old Testament Scripture Lesson (Ps. 51:8–12): Let me hear joy and gladness; let the bones that you have crushed rejoice. Hide your face from my sins, and blot out all my iniquities. Create in me a clean heart, O God, and put a new and right spirit within me. Do not cast me away from your presence, and do not take your holy spirit from me. Restore to me the joy of your salvation, and sustain in me a willing spirit. (Note: You will use all of Psalm 51 for the discussion.)

New Testament Scripture Lesson (Matt. 6:5–13): [Jesus said,] "And whenever you pray, do not be like the hypocrites;

for they love to stand and pray in the synagogues and at the street corners, so that they may be seen by others. Truly I tell you, they have received their reward. But whenever you pray, go into your room and shut the door and pray to your Father who is in secret; and your Father who sees in secret will reward you.

"When you are praying, do not heap up empty phrases as the Gentiles do; for they think that they will be heard because of their many words. Do not be like them, for your Father knows what you need before you ask him.

"Pray then in this way: Our Father in heaven, hallowed be your name. Your kingdom come. Your will be done, on earth as it is in heaven. Give us this day our daily bread. And forgive us our debts, as we also have forgiven our debtors. And do not bring us to the time of trial, but rescue us from the evil one. (Note: You can also read Luke 11:1–4.)

Bart's Prayer

Well, old-timer, I guess this is the end of the road. I know I haven't always been a good kid, but if I have to go to school tomorrow, I'll fail the test and be held back. I just need one more day to study, Lord. I need your help . . . a teacher's strike, a power failure, a blizzard—anything that will cancel school tomorrow. I know that it's asking a lot, but if anyone can do it, you can. Thanking you in advance, your pal, Bart Simpson.

Activity: Have each person in your group take about ten minutes to write down a prayer that would represent how he or she would pray on any typical day. Encourage group members to think carefully about what is included in their most common prayers and to make this prayer reflect the form that their prayers most often take. When everyone is finished, have volunteers share the prayers they wrote and talk about the most important elements of their prayers.

Questions for Discussion: Prior to the discussion, have a member of the group read each of the Scripture lessons.

• Ask the group the following questions: Why do you pray? How often do you pray? When do you pray? Do you pray out loud, like Bart, or silently?

• Have participants analyze the prayers they wrote. What elements are most common among all the prayers?

• Have participants compare their prayers to Bart's prayer. How are they similar? How are they different?

• What are the priorities reflected in Bart's prayer? What priorities are reflected in the prayers of the group?

• Have participants open their Bibles to the Lord's Prayer as it appears in Matthew 6:9–13. Does Bart's prayer have anything in common with the Lord's Prayer? (Bart's prayer acknowledges the holiness of God and reflects a personal relationship with God. It also begins with confession ["I know I haven't always been a good kid"] and expresses gratitude ["Thanking you in advance, your pal, Bart Simpson"]. While Bart's prayer has a fundamentally selfish intent, it does express the needs of the day and leaves the response to those needs in God's hands.)

• Have participants open their Bibles to Psalm 51. How is Bart's prayer fundamentally different from King David's most famous prayer? Does Bart's prayer have anything in common with this great prayer? (Again, Bart's prayer is fundamentally selfish and, on the surface, concerns itself with something that could be viewed as trivial. Yet both prayers build on confession in order to ask God for deliverance.)

• Does Bart's prayer put God to the test? (Yes, in that Bart assumes that God will hear the prayer and acknowledge it with a sign. On the other hand, if God doesn't deliver, then Bart will interpret that as the indifference of God to his plight [another important theme in the Psalms].)

- Lisa overhears Bart praying and comments, "Prayer—the last refuge of a scoundrel." What do you think she means? (Bart's prayer is basically prayed in desperation at the last possible minute. Lisa feels that there is much that Bart could have done himself to avoid the situation in which he finds himself. She sees Bart using God as a "safety valve" or a "court of last resort.")

> **Lisa:** I heard you last night, Bart. You prayed for this. Now your prayers have been answered. I'm no theologian. I don't know who or what God is exactly. All I know is that he's a force more powerful than Mom and Dad put together and you owe him big.
>
> **Bart:** You're right. I asked for a miracle and I got it. I've got to study, man.

- Do you believe that the snowstorm came as a "miracle" in answer to Bart's prayer, or was it just a "divine coincidence"?

- Do you believe that God miraculously re-orders the universe in response to our prayers, or do our prayers prepare us to understand God's will in the "big picture"?

- How do you think Bart would have responded if his prayer had not been answered?

- Have you ever experienced what you feel to be unanswered prayer?

- Does God occasionally say no to our prayers?

- How do you think God responds when we pray for something that is not in our best interest?

- Bart is about to head out into the snow to play when Lisa catches him and reminds him of his promise. What key role is Lisa playing here? (We all need people who are willing to hold us accountable for our spiritual commitments. Lisa tradition-ally takes this role, not just for Bart but for the whole family.)

• At the end of the episode, Bart says, "Part of this D minus belongs to God." Who else contributes to Bart's passing grade? (Bart himself did study and got the extra point due to his effort. His teacher was understanding, flexible, and merciful to him. His family was loving and supportive through it all. Lisa called him into accountability. The ultimate answer to Bart's prayer is a combination of important factors that all work together for his good.)

Prayer: O Lord, teach us how to pray. We know that prayer is the foundation of our relationship with you. We want to be in conversation with you each and every day of our lives. Help us to find the time to pray and to learn to pray in appropriate ways. Amen.

Something to Talk About: This week find time to talk to someone you respect about the importance of prayer in his or her life. Ask this person, "Why do you pray? How often do you pray? When do you pray? What form do your prayers take?

Three

Skepticism and Blind Faith

Episode: "Lisa the Skeptic"
(*Trick or Treehouse*, vol. 3: *Heaven and Hell*)

Synopsis: When a development company breaks ground for a new mall, Lisa is concerned that an archaeological survey has not been done in the area. The developers agree to allow the survey, and Lisa volunteers to lead the expedition. During the dig an artifact is discovered that appears to be a human skeleton with wings. People automatically assume that it is the skeleton of an angel. Lisa, however, doubts that this is true and seeks a rational, scientific explanation for the find. Homer sets the skeleton up in a makeshift shrine in his garage, and the people of Springfield flock to see it. In the end, the skeleton turns out to be a hoax designed to promote the new mall.

Supplementary Reading: Chapter 3 of *The Gospel according to The Simpsons*

Old Testament Scripture Lesson (Prov. 14:15): The simple believe everything, but the clever consider their steps.

New Testament Scripture Lesson (John 20:24–29): But Thomas (who was called the Twin), one of the twelve, was not with them when Jesus came. So the other disciples told him, "We have seen the Lord." But he said to them, "Unless I see the mark of the nails in his hands, and put my finger in the mark of the nails and my hand in his side, I will not believe."

A week later his disciples were again in the house, and Thomas was with them. Although the doors were shut, Jesus came and stood among them and said, "Peace be with you." Then he said to Thomas, "Put your finger here and see my hands. Reach out your hand and put it in my side. Do not doubt but believe." Thomas answered him, "My Lord and my God!" Jesus said to him, "Have you believed because you have seen me? Blessed are those who have not seen and yet have come to believe."

(Heb. 11:1): Now faith is the assurance of things hoped for, the conviction of things not seen.

? What Is a Skeptic?

A skeptic is a person who doubts, questions, or suspends judgment on ideas generally accepted by others. A skeptic is not easily persuaded or convinced and often has to see evidence that confirms an idea before he or she will believe that it is true. As a philosophy, skepticism holds that the truth of all we know should be questioned and that doubting is the most important step in any intellectual process. Skepticism has come to be associated by many with doubting the fundamental doctrines and principles of religions, especially Christianity.

Activity: Make sure the group understands what a skeptic is, then ask members to take about five minutes to make a list of ideas about which they are skeptical. This list could include, but not be limited to, UFOs, the Loch Ness Monster, the Abominable Snowman, the Bermuda Triangle, the existence of Atlantis, near-death experiences, reincarnation, communication beyond death, psychics, or fortune telling. After they are done creating their lists, discuss the ideas and why they cause skepticism. What would it take to make a person believe that one of these ideas is true?

Questions for Discussion: Prior to the discussion, have a member of the group read aloud each of the Scripture lessons.

- Why do you think that the people are so quick to believe that the skeleton uncovered at the dig is an angel? (Some people are quick to believe anything that will support their spiritual worldview. In many ways, they are the opposite of skeptics in that it is easy for them to believe and they do not require proof before they accept an idea.)

- Do you believe in angels? If so, what convinced you to believe?

- What are some possible reasons to doubt the skeleton's authenticity? (Angels are spiritual beings created by God to live on a different plane of existence. It is doubtful that an angel would have a skeleton like ours.)

- When Homer sets the skeleton up in the makeshift shrine in his garage, Lisa says, "It's not fair to claim this thing is an angel. There's no proof of that." Lisa seems to be the only person who doubts. What does Lisa suggest they should do to help decide what the skeleton is? (She wants to take it to the museum and have it analyzed by scientists. She places her confidence in science.)

- Lisa says, "I took a piece of the skeleton for scientific analysis; soon we'll have all the facts." Are facts the only reason to believe that something is true?

- Homer responds to Lisa, "Facts are meaningless. You can use facts to prove anything that's even remotely true." Homer seems to have a "blind faith" that will allow him to ignore the facts in light of what he believes. How do you feel about this attitude?

- When the scientific tests come back inconclusive, Reverend Lovejoy says, "Science has faltered once again in the face of overwhelming religious evidence." Do science and faith always have to be at odds?

- When she appears on television, Lisa says, "You can either accept science and face reality, or you can believe in angels and live in a childish dream world." Are there reasons to believe in angels that have nothing to do with science? Is Lisa being fair to people who believe in angels as part of their faith?

- Is it fair—or respectful—to question someone else's faith or doctrine if it is different from your own?

- Ned Flanders says, "Science is like a blabbermouth who ruins a movie by telling you how it ends. Well I say there are some things we don't want to know—important things." Are there some things you don't want to know or is your faith strong enough to stand up to skepticism?

- Read Proverbs 14:15 again. What does this verse have to say about being skeptical? (This verse indicates that it is wise to consider your steps before believing something is true.)

- When Lisa is talking to her mother, she says, "What grown person could believe in angels?" to which Marge replies, "Your mother, for one." She goes on to tell Lisa, "There has to be more to life than just what we see. If you can't make a leap of faith now and then, I feel sorry for you." What does this say about Marge's faith? Do you think what she says has an impact on Lisa? (Lisa responds, "It's not that I don't have a spiritual side. I just find it hard to believe there's a dead angel hanging in our garage.")

- Read Hebrews 11:1 again. Discuss Marge's comments to Lisa based on the definition of faith offered by the author of Hebrews.

- Refer back to the story of Thomas's encounter with the resurrected presence of Jesus (John 20:24–29). What does this story have to say about skepticism and faith? Is Lisa like Thomas? (Thomas refused to believe that Jesus had risen from the dead until he could actually see Jesus and touch his wounds. Jesus did not condemn Thomas for his skepticism, but simply allowed him to prove to himself that Jesus had indeed risen from the dead. This story indicates that skepticism and doubts often lead us to a deeper sense of acceptance and faith.)

- When the hoax is uncovered, Lisa says to the developers, "You exploited peoples' deepest beliefs just to hawk your cheesy wares." What does this have to say about Lisa? (Despite her skepticism, Lisa respects the beliefs of others.)

Prayer: Our heavenly Creator, we confess that occasionally we have doubts. Sometimes it's hard to just accept the things we believe on faith alone. Help us to remember that faith is about believing in things that often cannot be proved. Help us to transcend our doubts and have faith in you. Amen.

Something to Talk About: Find time this week to talk to a scientist or science teacher you respect about the relationship between faith and science. Does this person see a contradiction between faith and science, or has he or she found a way to make science and faith work together?

Four

When Bad Things Happen to Good People

Episode: "When Flanders Failed"
(*The Best of* The Simpsons, vol. 10)

S ynopsis: Ned Flanders holds a neighborhood barbecue at which he announces that he is leaving his job to go into business. Ned plans to open a store at the mall called "The Leftorium," which will specialize in items for left-handed persons. When Homer shows up at the barbecue, he and Ned break a wishbone. Homer wishes for Ned's business to fail miserably. When The Leftorium begins to fail, Homer delights in Ned's misfortune. In the end, however, Homer has a change of heart and makes it possible for Ned to recover his losses by spreading the news about the store and Ned's plight to others.

Supplementary Reading: Chapter 4 of *The Gospel according to* The Simpsons

Old Testament Scripture Lesson (Ps. 13:1–6): How long, O LORD? Will you forget me forever? How long will you hide your face from me? How long must I bear pain in my soul, and have sorrow in my heart all day long? How long shall my enemy be exalted over me? Consider and answer me, O LORD my God! Give light to my eyes, or I will sleep the sleep of death, and my enemy will say, "I have prevailed"; my foes will rejoice because I am shaken. But I trusted in your steadfast love; my heart shall rejoice in your salvation. I will sing to the LORD, because he has dealt bountifully with me.

New Testament Scripture Lesson (Rom. 5:1–5): Therefore, since we are justified by faith, we have peace with God through our Lord Jesus Christ, through whom we have obtained access to this grace in which we stand; and we boast in our hope of sharing the glory of God. And not only that, but we also boast in our sufferings, knowing that suffering produces endurance, and endurance produces character, and character produces hope, and hope does not disappoint us, because God's love has been poured into our hearts through the Holy Spirit that has been given to us.

Activity: Have group members each take about five minutes to write down what they consider to be the worst day in their lives. When they are finished, have volunteers share their worst day with the group. Ask the group the following questions: What caused this to be such a bad day? What was the source of your suffering? Did the situation improve? What helped you to transcend your bad day?

Questions for Discussion: Prior to the discussion, have a member of the group read aloud each of the Scripture lessons.

- Homer wishes for Ned's business to fail. Do you think Homer's wish *causes* Ned's business to fail?

- Should a person of faith believe in curses or bad luck?

- Have you ever wished for something bad to happen to another person? Do you know someone who has?

- Is it possible that Ned's business fails because it was a bad idea to begin with?

- What are some of the other factors that lead to Ned's failure? (Ned is far too lenient with his customers. He allows them to take advantage of him. He doesn't ask people to pay for items they break. He validates parking tickets without a purchase. He also fails to promote the store to the public.)

- Lisa introduces Homer to the concept of "shameful joy," or taking pleasure in the suffering of others. Why does Homer delight in Ned's suffering? (Homer is jealous of the respect and admiration Ned receives from others. Ned approaches life with joyful gratitude and Homer finds Ned's positive outlook on life irritating. He feels that if Ned fails he will become more pessimistic.)

- Does the suffering Ned experiences cause him to be more pessimistic? (Ned gets discouraged, but never seems to lose his positive outlook on life.)

- Does suffering make you more pessimistic, or are you able to find reasons to be positive even in the worst circumstances?

- Read Psalm 13:1–6 again. Do you think that Ned feels the same way that the psalmist does? Do you sometimes feel like God has abandoned you or doesn't hear your prayers?

- How do you feel about "calling God out" the way the psalmist does? Do you think God understands our discouragement, frustration, and impatience in times of suffering?

- After Homer and Bart buy out the Flanderses' desperation garage sale, Lisa says to Bart, "I'm sure you did nothing to discourage this, you scavenger of human misery." Homer and Bart willingly take advantage of Ned and his family during a time of suffering. Do we sometimes take advantage of other peoples' failures?

- Ned loses everything, including his house, yet he chooses to keep a positive frame of mind. Do you know people like Ned who continue to be at their best even when things are at their worst?

- When faced with the prospect of being homeless and sleeping in their car, the Flanderses sing "Put on a Happy Face." Why aren't they more miserable? (It's a matter of attitude. While on the surface this may seem ridiculous, the Flanderses choose not to allow suffering to conquer their spirit.)

- What gives the Flanderses the strength to persevere? (The Flanderses have their faith to support them.)

- Read Romans 5:1–5 again. What does Paul have to say about the effects of suffering? (Paul lists a set of conditions: "Suffering produces endurance, and endurance produces character, and character produces hope." Paul believes that the end result of suffering for people of faith is hope. Hope is then the foundation for each of us to transcend our suffering.)

- Are Ned Flanders and his family a living embodiment of Romans 5:1–5?

- Ned says to Homer, "I'm ruined. You know at times like these I used to turn to the Bible and find solace, but even the good book can't help me now." Because Ned sold his Bible to Homer in the yard sale for seven cents, he doesn't have a Bible to read. Ned's first impulse in a time of suffering is to turn to the Bible. How can the Bible help us in times of suffering?

- Despite the fact that Homer has been wishing him ill behind the scenes, Ned calls Homer a "true friend" for trying to warn him that the store would fail. What does this have to say about Ned's outlook on life? (It would be easy to say that Ned is naïve, but he is really the kind of person who looks for the best in everybody.)

- Homer finally comes around and helps Ned out of his dilemma. What has changed for Homer? (Homer has seen Ned through the eyes of compassion. He is able to empathize with Ned. Throughout it all, Homer is basically a good person who is subject to many human frailties.)

- What saves Ned in the end? (The community comes forward in response to his need. Ned has given of himself to the community, and the community comes forward to support him.)

- Does being part of a faith community help you in times of suffering?

Prayer: Lord, we know that sometimes bad things can happen to good people. We know that our faith commitment does not protect us from experiencing suffering and pain. Guide us through our times of suffering and pain and help us to depend on you when we are hurting the most. Show us ways to alleviate pain and suffering wherever we find it in the world. Amen.

Something to Talk About: Find time this week to talk to someone you respect about a time when he or she suffered. How did this person deal with the suffering? How did this person's faith commitment prepare him or her to encounter a time of suffering?

Five

What Is a Soul?

Episode: "Bart Sells His Soul"
(*Trick or Treat Treehouse*, vol. 3: *Heaven and Hell*)

Synopsis: When Bart plays a prank at church, Milhouse tattles on him and they both are assigned the duty of cleaning out the organ pipes as punishment. When Bart asks Milhouse why he tattled, Milhouse confesses that he thought his soul would be in jeopardy if he lied. Bart contends that there is no such thing as a soul and offers to sell his soul to Milhouse for five dollars. Milhouse agrees and takes possession of a sheet of paper with "Bart Simpson's Soul" written on it. Bart then begins to discover the consequences of his action and does everything he can to regain his soul.

Supplementary Reading: Chapter 6 of *The Gospel according to The Simpsons*

Old Testament Scripture Lesson (Ps. 25:1): To you, O LORD, I lift up my soul.
(Ps. 42:1–6): As a deer longs for flowing streams, so my soul longs for you, O God. My soul thirsts for God, for the living God. When shall I come and behold the face of God? My tears have been my food day and night, while people say to me continually, "Where is your God?"

These things I remember, as I pour out my soul: how I went with the throng, and led them in procession to the house of God, with glad shouts and songs of thanksgiving, a multitude keeping festival. Why are you cast down, O my soul, and why are you disquieted within me? Hope in God; for I shall again praise him, my help and my God.

New Testament Scripture Lesson (Matt. 10:28): Do not fear those who kill the body but cannot kill the soul; rather fear him who can destroy both soul and body in hell.
(1 Cor. 15:51–55): Listen, I will tell you a mystery! We will not all die, but we will all be changed, in a moment, in the twinkling of an eye, at the last trumpet. For the trumpet will sound, and the dead will be raised imperishable, and we will be changed. For this perishable body must put on imperishability, and this mortal body must put on immortality. When this perishable body puts on imperishability, and this mortal body puts on immortality, then the saying that is written will be fulfilled: "Death has been swallowed up in victory." "Where, O death, is your victory? Where, O death, is your sting?"

☀ The Simpsons on the Soul

- Your soul is the most valuable part of you.

- Whether or not the soul is physically real, it's the symbol of everything fine inside.

- Your soul is the only part of you that lasts forever.

- Some philosophers believe that nobody is born with a soul; that you have to earn one through suffering and thought and prayer.

Activity: Have each person in the group take about five minutes to write his or her own answer to the question, "What is a soul?" When everyone has finished, ask volunteers to share their definitions. Have the group compare their definitions to the statements *The Simpsons* makes about the soul. Make a list of the most important aspects of the soul that are revealed in the groups' answers.

Questions for Discussion: Prior to the discussion, have a member of the group read aloud each of the Scripture lessons.

- The controversy about the soul begins when Reverend Lovejoy has the children repeat the following: "If I withhold the truth may I go straight to hell, where I will eat naught but burning hot coals and drink naught but burning hot cola. Where fiery demons will brush me in the back. Where my soul will be chopped into confetti and strewn on a parade of murderers and single mothers. Where my tongue will be torn out by ravenous birds." This is obviously meant by the show's writers to be humorous, but how do you feel about "fire and brimstone" threats like these?

- What do you believe about hell? Is it a place where souls will be punished physically as suggested by Reverend Lovejoy?

- When asked by Bart why he tattled, Milhouse replies, "I didn't want hungry birds pecking my soul forever." How do you feel about people using the fear of eternal punishment as a motivation for actions in this life? Does God want us to turn to God out of fear?

- Bart says, "Soul—come on, Milhouse, there's no such thing as the soul. It's just something they made up to scare kids, like the Boogie Man or Michael Jackson." Do you know anyone who agrees with Bart? Do you think there are many people who don't believe in the existence of the soul?

- How would you respond if someone challenged the existence of the soul as Bart has? What would be your arguments to defend its existence?

- Milhouse says, "But every religion says there's a soul, Bart. Why would they lie? What would they have to gain?" The scene then changes to Reverend Lovejoy counting the offering money. Do you think the church has used peoples' concern for the fate of their souls as a way of maintaining power? Can the church abuse that kind of power?

- When Bart asks Milhouse, "If the soul's real, where is it?" Milhouse points to his heart and says, "It's in here." How do we know we have a soul? How does our faith confirm its existence?

- Bart and Milhouse have a discussion about the soul in which Milhouse expresses some childish notions. For instance, he suggests that when we sneeze, our soul is trying to get out, and saying "God bless you" crams it back in. He also maintains that the soul can swim (in case you die in a submarine) and has wheels (in case you die in the desert). Did you have different notions about the soul when you were a child? Do we need to do a better job teaching children about the idea of the soul?

- Bart sells his soul to Milhouse. Do you think it is actually possible to sell your soul?

- Read Matthew 10:28 again. Jesus tells the disciples that "both soul and body" can be destroyed and that this is something they should fear. How do you feel about that idea? How would you relate it to Bart's plight?

- When Lisa discovers Bart has sold his soul, she says, "Whether or not the soul is physically real, it's the symbol of everything fine inside us." How do you feel about Lisa's assessment of the concept of soul?

- Read Psalm 25:1 again. How does the psalmist view his soul? (The psalmist sees his soul as the part of him that is in direct relationship with God.)

- Bart offers to sell Lisa his conscience and sense of decency. What is the difference between these concepts and the idea of soul? (No one has ever suggested that our conscience or sense of decency are separate entities that last forever. However, some people feel our conscience and sense of decency are tied to our soul along with our free will.)

- What convinces Bart that his soul is actually missing? (The dog and cat growl and hiss. The automatic door doesn't open. His breath won't fog the glass on the ice cream freezer. His mom senses that something is missing in his hug. It's funny to think that the absence of a soul would have physical consequences.)

- Do you believe that the absence of a soul would have physical effects that could be sensed by others? (Whether or not we believe that the absence of a soul can have these effects, they certainly convince Bart that his soul is missing.)

- One of the signs that Bart's soul is missing is the fact that he can't laugh. Lisa quotes Pablo Neruda to him, "Laughter is the language of the soul." What do you think Neruda was trying to say?

- Take some time to discuss Bart's dreams about his soul (or the lack thereof). What parts of the dream do you think reflect people's actual ideas about the soul?

- Bart struggles to get his soul back, and when all else fails he prays, "Are you there God? It's me, Bart Simpson. I know I never paid much attention in church, but I could really use some of that good stuff now. I'm afraid—I'm afraid some weirdo has got my soul and I don't know what they're doing to it. I just want it back, please. I hope you can hear this." Do you think this is an appropriate prayer? (Like many of the psalms in which the psalmist prays for deliverance, Bart acknowledges his concern that God will hear his prayer. He confesses his failures and expresses his fears. He acknowledges his human frailty in being unable to accomplish his purpose and recover his lost soul. He expresses his dependence on God for any potential outcome.)

- Are Bart's prayers answered? (Bart's prayers are answered when Lisa presents him with the paper bearing "his soul." She had done the loving thing and bought it back for him.)

- Read 1 Corinthians 15:51–55 again. What do these verses have to say about the nature and existence of the soul? (This is one place in the Bible where the survival of a part of us after death is discussed directly. Paul draws no conclusions about the nature and existence of the soul, but emphasizes the mystical reality of the change that takes place when we die. Paul may not have been able to describe "the soul" in concrete terms, but he believes that part of us goes on to imperishability and immortality after we die.)

- Lisa observes, "Some philosophers believe that nobody is born with a soul, that you have to earn one through suffering and thought and prayer." How do you feel about this concept of the soul?

Prayer: Our Lord and Redeemer, our souls look up to you. We know that you have created us and breathed into us the breath of life. Guide us as we seek to live as those who bear your divine image. Help us to prepare ourselves for an eternity in your love. Amen.

Something to Talk About: Find time this week to talk to someone you respect about what he or she believes about his or her soul.

Six

Little Sins and Big Sins

Episode: "Homer vs. Lisa and the Eighth Commandment"
(*The Best of* The Simpsons, vol. 8)

Synopsis: When Homer overhears Ned Flanders driving off a cable television installer who is offering to hook the Flanderses up illegally for fifty dollars with no monthly payments to follow, he chases after the man and has him hook up the Simpson household. When his family comes home, he proudly announces that the Simpsons have cable. At first Marge questions the legality of the arrangement, but gets sucked in while watching the women's channel. That weekend in Lisa's Sunday school class, the lesson is about hell and the Ten Commandments. Lisa, fearing her family is hell-bound for breaking the Eighth Commandment, begins to protest the illegal hookup in hopes that Homer and her family will see the light. In the end, Homer reluctantly agrees to do the right thing and cuts the cable.

Supplementary Reading: Chapter 7 of *The Gospel according to* The Simpsons

Old Testament Scripture Lesson (Exod. 20:15): You shall not steal.
(Lev. 19:11): You shall not steal; you shall not deal falsely; and you shall not lie to one another.

New Testament Scripture Lesson (Rom. 2:21–23): You, then, that teach others, will you not teach yourself? While you preach against stealing, do you steal? You that forbid adultery, do you commit adultery? You that abhor idols, do you rob temples? You that boast in the law, do you dishonor God by breaking the law?

Questions for Discussion: Prior to the discussion, have a member of the group read aloud each of the Scripture lessons.

- Homer knows that receiving cable without paying the monthly premium is against the law. Why is he so anxious to do it anyway? (Homer caves in to temptation and rationalizes the cable theft. He doesn't feel that cable theft is that big of a deal.)

- The cable installer who hooks up Homer illegally gives Homer a book entitled *So You've Decided to Steal Cable.* The first thing Homer reads is, "Myth: Cable piracy is wrong. Fact: Cable companies are big faceless corporations, which makes it O.K." Do you think many people rationalize the theft of cable this way? Is it easier to steal from a "big faceless corporation" than from another person?

- Is there such a thing as a "victimless crime" or "victimless sin?" Who is the victim in the case of cable theft? (In order to provide cable, the cable company must charge those who receive it. The loss of revenue from cable theft is then passed on to other customers, which raises their monthly premiums.)

- Homer seems to believe in the idea that there is a difference between "big sins" and "little sins." At one point he says to Marge, "There are thieves everywhere and I'm not talking about the small forgivable stuff." Do you think there is a difference between "big sins" and "little sins," or are all sins the same in the eyes of God?

- Read Exodus 20:15 and Leviticus 19:11 again. Does God differentiate between different degrees of sin in regard to stealing? (No, God is clear that any degree of theft would fall under his commandment not to steal.)

- Is there a difference between sins committed against God and sins committed against other people? Does God forgive both kinds?

- Are some sins unforgivable? (When this question is asked, someone will inevitably bring up Mark 3:29: "But whoever blasphemes against the Holy Spirit can never have forgiveness, but is guilty of an eternal sin." One way to explain this is to say that if one does not believe in the Holy Spirit then one cannot ask for forgiveness. However, it is best to point out that God forgives all sin for those who sincerely seek God's grace.)

- Marge initially questions the legality of the cable hookup. What changes her mind? (Marge is tempted by a "women's channel" and rationalizes away her objections.)

- When the Sunday school teacher tells the class that the subject for discussion is hell, Bart says, "I've sat through mercy and I sat through forgiveness. Finally we get to the good stuff." Why do you think Bart finds mercy and forgiveness boring? Do you agree with him?

- The teacher describes hell as "a terrible place. Maggots are your sheet and worms your blanket. There's a lake of fire burning with sulfur. You'll be tormented day and night forever and ever. As a matter of fact, if you actually saw hell you'd be so frightened you would die." How do you feel about this literal description of hell as a physical reality?

- Bart asks about hell, "Wouldn't you eventually get used to it, like a hot tub?" Why do you think Bart doesn't take the concept of hell seriously? Do you think people today take the concept of hell seriously?

- One of the children asks, "So what you're saying is there's a downside to the afterlife. How does one steer clear of this abode of the damned?" What is the teacher's answer? (She says, "By obeying the Ten Commandments, ten simple rules that are easy to live by.")

- Do you agree that the Ten Commandments are "ten simple rules that are easy to live by"?

- Is obeying the Ten Commandments the way to salvation, or is there something else we must do? (Protestant Christians believe in salvation by grace through faith. We are saved by the grace of God, which is a gift freely given. While obeying the Ten Commandments is important to living a moral and ethical life, we can't "earn" our way to salvation through good works. The good works are a natural by-product of our commitment to God.)

- Lisa has a vision of her family in hell. Satan says to her, "Come on, Lisa, watch a little cable with us, it won't cost you anything—except your soul." She has obviously been frightened by her Sunday school class. Do you think God wants us to be motivated by fear?

- Lisa confronts Marge when she eats two grapes without paying for them at the grocery store. Do you think Lisa is going too far, or does she have a point?

- Marge eats the grapes without really thinking about it. Do you think there are some sins that we commit without really thinking about them?

- Lisa goes to her pastor, Reverend Lovejoy, for advice about her dilemma. She asks him, "So even if a man takes bread to feed his starving family that would be stealing?" Reverend Lovejoy replies, "No—well, it is if he puts anything on it—jelly, for example." What do you think Reverend Lovejoy is trying to say? (At first what Reverend Lovejoy says might seem silly, but he is suggesting that it is not stealing unless the man takes more than he needs to feed his family.)

- Do you agree with Reverend Lovejoy?

- Reverend Lovejoy makes the following suggestion: "Lisa, I would like to see you set an example by not watching the offending technology yourself." He is suggesting that Lisa attempt to change her family's attitude through her witness. Have you ever had an opportunity to witness in this way?

- Is Lisa's witness effective?

- How does Homer respond to Lisa's witness? (At first he tries to tempt her away with horse racing from Belmont [Lisa loves horses], but Lisa replies, "I'd rather go to heaven." Homer tries to ignore her, but she is obviously getting to him. Homer observes, "There's something wrong with that kid—she's so moral.")

- How does Lisa's witness affect the rest of her family? (Bart ignores her, but Marge is converted and tells Homer, "Lisa is losing respect for you.")

- Read Romans 2:21–23 again. What does the Bible have to say about the quality of our witness?

- What happens when Homer discovers Bart watching the adult channel? (Homer is aghast when he finds Bart watching the adult channel. He asks Bart not to watch, but, of course, Bart later charges admission for the neighborhood kids to see it. Homer hadn't anticipated the other possible consequences of getting cable.)

- Have you ever learned something in church or school that was in conflict with what you saw at home? Did that make you uncomfortable? How did you resolve it?

- Marge says, "When you love somebody, you have to have faith that in the end they will do the right thing." Have you ever had to have patience with somebody you loved who was doing the wrong thing? How did it turn out?

- How did Ned react to the offer of an illegal cable hookup? (Ned immediately turned the cable installer away. He refused to do something that was against his principles.)

- Have you ever been tempted to do something that was against your principles?

- Homer finally agrees to cut the cable and even joins his family on the lawn during the big fight. Lisa comments, "Dad, we may have saved your soul." To which Homer replies, "Yeah, at the worst possible moment." What does this have to say about Homer and doing the right thing? (Homer realizes that doing the right thing involves sacrifice, which he doesn't like. We often have to give something up to follow our principles, but principles are most important when they require us to give something up.)

Prayer: Our heavenly Creator, help us to live according to your commandments, not just for ourselves, but to be an example to others. Help us to remember that others are always watching us to see how we will react in certain situations. Show us the way to follow through on our spiritual principles by living out our faith in our everyday lives. Amen.

Something to Talk About: Find time this week to talk to someone you respect about the importance of witness. Ask this person how he or she sees himself or herself as an example in faith and what effect that witness has on others.

Seven

Lead Us Not into Temptation

Episode: "Life on the Fast Lane"
(*The Best of* The Simpsons, vol. 1)

Synopsis: When Homer forgets Marge's birthday, he rushes out to the mall to buy her a present. The present turns out to be a bowling ball drilled for Homer's fingers and engraved with his name. Marge is so angry at his insensitivity that she is determined to learn to bowl, even though she has never bowled in her life. At the bowling alley she meets Jacques, a hustler, who offers to give Marge bowling lessons. Jacques immediately begins attempting to seduce Marge, and she is taken in by the attention he gives her. Faced with a fork in the road, Marge chooses not to turn down the road to Jacques' apartment. Instead, she takes the other road and meets Homer at the nuclear power plant.

Supplementary Reading: Chapter 7 of *The Gospel according to* The Simpsons

Old Testament Scripture Lesson (Exod. 20:14): You shall not commit adultery.
(Prov. 6:32–33): But he who commits adultery has no sense; he who does it destroys himself. He will get wounds and dishonor, and his disgrace will not be wiped away.

New Testament Scripture Lesson (Jas. 1:12–16): Blessed is anyone who endures temptation. Such a one has stood the test and will receive the crown of life that the Lord has promised to those who love him. No one, when tempted, should say, "I am being tempted by God"; for God cannot be tempted by evil and he himself tempts no one. But one is tempted by one's own desire, being lured and enticed by it; then, when that desire has conceived, it gives birth to sin, and that sin, when it is fully grown, gives birth to death. Do not be deceived, my beloved.

Questions for Discussion: Prior to the discussion, have a member of the group read aloud each of the Scripture lessons.

- What leads to the tension between Marge and Homer? (Homer is inconsiderate and selfish. He forgets Marge's birthday and then buys a present intended for him rather than her.)

- At Marge's birthday dinner, Marge's sisters observe, "Thirty-four years old, time enough to start over with a new man." Why do they say this? (Marge's sisters have never liked Homer and never understood how Marge could have fallen in love with him. Of course, his behavior at the dinner does nothing to dispel their low opinion of him.)

- Why is Marge determined to learn to bowl? (For once she is going to turn the tables on Homer. She isn't going to let him get away with his selfishness. She decides to learn to bowl just to spite him.)

- Is Homer a good husband? Why or why not? (Homer is not sensitive to Marge's needs, but he tries to do the best he can. While she is at the bowling alley, he agrees to take care of the kids. As Marge spends more and more time bowling, Homer begins to understand what he is missing.)

- What is Marge missing from her marriage? (Homer is not very good at romance. He is insensitive and self-centered. He does not communicate well and doesn't make Marge feel valued. Homer makes no attempt to understand Marge's interests and needs.)

- Why does Marge seem to fall for Jacques? (Jacques gives her the attention that Homer never has. He focuses on her, even though his intent is selfish.)

- Why can we see that Jacques is a conman and a sleaze, but Marge cannot? (Marge relishes the attention. Part of her knows what's going on—she keeps saying, "But I'm a married woman"—but she is enjoying herself. Jacques makes her feel attractive and desired, so she is willing to look the other way.)

- What is special about Jacques' gift? (Jacques gets Marge her own bowling glove. It is her size and has her name embroidered on it. Jacques has done what Homer never has—given Marge a gift that is truly for her.)

- Jacques says of Marge's bowling ball, "Many people have sense-less attachments to heavy, clumsy things such as this Homer of yours." What is he really talking about? (Jacques is suggesting that Marge's marriage is a "senseless attachment." He wants to send Marge a message.)

- When does Homer realize that something is wrong in his marriage? (He begins to realize that something is wrong when Marge gets home late and informs him that she will be going bowling again the next day.)

- What does Lisa notice about the difference in her mother? (Lisa notices that Marge is overcompensating with her and Bart. When she makes them fabulous lunches full of special treats, Lisa says to Bart, "This is what psychologists call over-compensation. Mom is wracked with guilt because her marriage is failing.")

- What is Bart's response to Lisa's observation? (Bart is basically selfish. He says, "Don't rock the boat, man, whatever it is, we're making out like bandits." At first he doesn't seem to care about the problems his parents are having as long as he is getting something good out of the situation.)

- Lisa says, "I read about what happens to kids whose parents no longer love and cherish each other." What does she believe is going on with her and Bart? (She suggests that there are eight stages that children go through in these cases. She informs Bart that he is in stage two, denial, while she is in stage three, fear. Later she suggests that she has entered stage five, self-pity.)

- When does Bart realize that something is wrong? (When he goes out to play catch with Homer. He hits Homer in the head with the ball and Homer is too depressed to even say "Ouch." When Bart goes to Lisa in a panic she responds, "Welcome to stage three.")

- Have you ever dealt with a situation like this with your parents, someone you love, or someone you or a friend are dating?

- Are the standards for fidelity and faithfulness different when you are dating as opposed to being married? If so, how is the marriage covenant different from dating?

- Bart reminds Homer of advice that Homer once gave him. He says, "When something's bothering you and you're too . . . stupid to know what to do, just keep your fool mouth shut. At least that way you won't make things worse." Is this good advice? (No. It is exactly the opposite of what Homer needs to do. He needs to talk to Marge. One of the most important problems Marge and Homer face is a lack of communication.)

- Read James 1:12–16 again. What does this passage have to say about temptation? How does it apply to the situation in which Marge finds herself?

- Jacques asks Marge, "What cosmic force brought us together?" Do you think God had anything to do with Marge and Jacques getting together? (In James 1:12–16 the writer is clear that God tempts no one. God would not determine the situation that leads to Marge's temptation.)

- Marge has a fantasy about her meeting with Jacques at his apartment. What does this fantasy say about Marge's outlook on life? What part do you think our fantasies play in our being tempted? (Marge fantasizes about a perfect romantic evening. There is no way the evening could live up to the high expectations of her fantasy. In a fantasy, we can imagine the perfect outcome to following through on a temptation, but most of the time reality can never be as good as our fantasy.)

- Based on the James passage, what is the key component of temptation? How does this apply to Marge? (According to the passage, "One is tempted by one's own desire, being lured and enticed by it." It is Marge's desire to feel attractive and valued that leads to her temptation.)

- The Scripture says, "Blessed is anyone who endures temptation. Such a one has stood the test and will receive the crown of life that the Lord has promised to those who love him." Does Marge endure her temptation? (Despite being attracted to Jacques and even going as far as to schedule a meeting at his apartment, Marge perseveres and does the right thing in the end.)

- What helps Marge make the decision to resist temptation? (She is able to put things in perspective by thinking of how important her marriage and her family have been to her. On the way to Jacques' apartment she sees a wedding, families having fun together, and a couple growing old together. This leads her to contemplate the value of her relationships and the consequences of what she is doing.)

- Does Homer do anything that helps Marge resist temptation? (Marge sees how Homer is affected by what she has been doing. The morning of her scheduled meeting with Jacques, Homer compliments Marge on the way she makes peanut butter and jelly sandwiches. Even though the compliment concerns something that seems silly and trivial, Marge takes notice that Homer cares for her in his own way.)

- When Marge is at brunch with Jacques, Helen Lovejoy (Reverend Lovejoy's wife) sees them and comes over to speak to them. Does she act out of friendship? (Helen Lovejoy is a gossip, and when she sees Marge "having brunch with a man who isn't your husband," she wants Marge to know that she has seen her. While Helen doesn't judge Marge openly, she is certainly calling Marge's actions into question. A true friend would find the appropriate time to talk about what might be going on in Marge's life.)

• How can our friends help us deal with temptation? (Having people we trust is essential to dealing with temptation. We need someone to whom we can talk, someone who will help us deal with our temptations openly. A dedicated friend will hold us accountable for our actions and help us to make good, objective decisions.)

• Have volunteers from the group share stories about times when they found themselves tempted and how they dealt with their temptations.

Prayer: Our Lord and our God, often we find ourselves tempted by worldly desires. We know that this is part of what it means to be a human being. Help us to avoid temptation whenever it is possible. When we cannot avoid temptation, we ask you to give us the strength to encounter our temptations with our faith. Amen.

Something to Talk About: Find time this week to talk to someone you respect about temptation. What part does temptation play in this person's life, and how does he or she deal with temptation through faith?

Eight

How We See the Bible

Episode: "Simpsons Bible Stories"
(At present this episode is commercially unavailable. Check with your
Fox television affiliate for broadcast times so you can watch it as a group.
You may also want to view again the opening sequence to
"Homer vs. Lisa and the Eighth Commandment.")

Synopsis: When Reverend Lovejoy begins reading from the
Bible during worship, the Simpsons are bored and each of them
falls asleep in turn. While sleeping they each dream they are part of
a Bible story. Marge dreams that she and Homer are Adam and Eve
in the garden of Eden. Lisa dreams that she is Moses' "right hand
woman" during the exodus. Homer dreams he is Solomon. Bart
dreams that he is King David having to deal with Goliath's son.

Supplementary Reading: Chapter 8 of *The Gospel according to
The Simpsons*

Old Testament Scripture Lesson (Ps. 119:103–106): How
sweet are your words to my taste, sweeter than honey to my
mouth! Through your precepts I get understanding; therefore I
hate every false way. Your word is a lamp to my feet and a light to
my path. I have sworn an oath and confirmed it, to observe your
righteous ordinances.

New Testament Scripture Lesson (2 Tim. 3:14–17): But as for
you, continue in what you have learned and firmly believed,
knowing from whom you learned it, and how from childhood you
have known the sacred writings that are able to instruct you for
salvation through faith in Christ Jesus. All scripture is inspired by

---

📖 Four Ways of Looking at the Bible

1. The Bible is the literal word of God. What we find in the Bible is exactly what God dictated to the biblical writers. Because the Bible is the exact word of God, it contains no errors or inconsistencies, and no part of the Bible is more important than any other part. Everything in the Bible must be read literally and means exactly what it says.

2. The Bible is the inspired word of God. God inspired the writers of the Bible, but they were human beings and wrote the books themselves. God did not dictate to them every word they wrote. The writers were from different times in history, and their writing reflects their view of God and the view of the world of their time. Because they were inspired by God, they each communicate spiritual truth, but because they were human, some inconsistencies can be found in their writing. These inconsistencies don't make a difference, however, because we are not always reading the Bible literally. This also means that some parts of the Bible can be more important than others. The Bible is the word of God communicated to us by human beings who had special relationships with God.

3. The word of God can be found in the Bible. The Bible is a collection of stories that tell us about the nature of God. In these stories the word of God can be found, but the Bible was never meant to be accepted as literal or historical truth. Some parts of the Bible are irrelevant for our time because they reflect world outlooks from different cultures at different times in history. The word of God comes to us through our interpretation of the Scriptures. We must question the Bible in order to glean the word of God from the writings it contains.

4. The Bible is a "good book." The Bible is just a "good book" that gives good moral, ethical, and spiritual advice. It is not inspired by God in any way.

God and is useful for teaching, for reproof, for correction, and for training in righteousness, so that everyone who belongs to God may be proficient, equipped for every good work.

Activity: Take about five minutes for members of the group to write down a time when the Bible has been important to them. When they have finished, have volunteers share what they have written and discuss how the Bible influences their lives.

Questions for Discussion: Prior to the discussion, have a member of the group read aloud each of the Scripture lessons.

• Share the four ways of looking at the Bible with the group. Which way of looking at the Bible is closest to your view?

• Do you believe that the Bible is the exact word of God and contains no errors or inconsistencies?

• How do you deal with inconsistencies found in the Bible?

• What part does your faith play in the way you view the Bible?

• Read 2 Timothy 3:14–17 again. What do you think Paul meant when he said to Timothy, "All scripture is inspired by God?" (The Greek word for *inspired* means "God breathed." It bears the same connotation as when God made human beings from the dust and breathed life into them.)

• Read Psalm 119:103–106 again. What place does the psalmist suggest the Bible should have in our lives?

• In one episode of *The Simpsons*, when Reverend Lovejoy is being judgmental, Lisa quotes Matthew 7:1: "Judge not, lest ye be judged." Reverend Lovejoy replies that while that may be in the Bible, he's sure that it is "somewhere towards the back." Reverend Lovejoy is insinuating that certain parts of the Bible are more important than others. Do you agree with him?

• If you believe that certain parts of the Bible are more important than others, what parts are the most important? What parts are the least important?

- Do you know anyone who thinks the Bible is just a "good book" that gives good moral, ethical, and spiritual advice and is not inspired by God in any way? How would you respond to a person who sees the Bible that way?

- On *The Simpsons*, characters often quote from the Bible, but they also often get the quotes wrong. Do you feel this is a misrepresentation of the Bible?

- Do you know anyone who misquotes the Bible or uses parts of the Bible out of context to defend his or her position?

- In "Simpsons Bible Stories," each of the characters dreams a humorous version of one of the stories from the Bible. Does it make you uncomfortable when the *The Simpsons* uses the Bible in a humorous way, or do you think it makes a point about how society views the Bible?

- Should the Bible be the target of satirical humor, or should it be viewed in a more sacred way?

- Marge is the first to have a dream. She dreams she is Eve in the garden of Eden, with Homer as Adam. From what you remember of the story of Adam and Eve, talk about the differences between *The Simpsons*' version and the real thing. (The list could include but not be limited to: Eve appears first even though she was not created first. God is played by Ned Flanders. When God tells them not to eat from the tree of knowledge Homer/Adam replies that the temptation to eat from the tree would be easier to resist if he had a few more wives. The pig has conversations with them and provides pork without dying. Homer/Adam eats from the fruit of the tree of knowledge first. Marge/Eve follows his lead because "it is a sin to waste food." Because Homer/Adam refuses to support her, God kicks only Eve out of the garden at first. Homer/Adam sneaks Marge/Eve back into the garden. If you wish to compare the two stories in more detail, the story of Adam and Eve is found in Genesis 2:4–3:24.)

- In this story, Homer/Adam tries to talk God out of banishing them from the garden by arguing, "God is love, right?" Is this New Testament idea of God in conflict with the Old Testament idea of God?

- Once they are out of the garden, Marge/Eve argues, "I'm sure God will let us return soon. How long can he hold a grudge?" Do you think of God as holding grudges?

- Lisa dreams that she is Moses' "right hand woman" during the exodus. From what you remember of the story of Moses and the exodus, talk about the differences between *The Simpsons'* version and the real thing. (The list could include but not be limited to: The slaves are all children. Lisa takes the role of Aaron, Moses' brother who spoke for him. The burning bush tattles on Bart. The plague of frogs is produced by a trip to the market. The plague doesn't have the desired effect, as Pharaoh enjoys eating frog legs. The parting of the Red Sea is created by the simultaneous flushing of toilets. Moses wavers in his faith, saved from converting to the Egyptian god Ra by Lisa. If you wish to compare the two stories in more detail, the story of the exodus begins with the fifth chapter of the book of Exodus.)

- Homer dreams that he is King Solomon. From what you remember of the story of King Solomon, talk about the differences between the *The Simpsons'* version and the real thing. (The list could include but not be limited to: Homer's dream reflects his self-centered nature. He dreams he is King Solomon deciding between two men who claim ownership of the same pie. He cuts the pie in half, sentences the men to death and then eats the pie himself. The story of King Solomon and the baby is about justice and Homer commits a grave injustice. There is also a scene in which Jesus comes before him to have a case decided. How do you feel about that? Is it offensive? If you wish to compare the two stories in more detail, the story of King Solomon deciding between the two mothers who claimed the same baby can be found in 1 Kings 3:16–28.)

- Bart dreams that he is King David preparing to fight Golaith's son. From what you remember of the story of David and Goliath, talk about the differences between *The Simpsons'* version and the real thing. (There is virtually nothing in this story that bears any resemblance to a biblical story of David. David's attitude is changed from arrogance to humility, but that is the only similarity to any of the stories of David. Bart's dream is a combination of championship wrestling and "Jack and the Beanstalk." The actual story of David and Goliath can be found in the seventeenth chapter of 1 Samuel.)

- When the Simpsons wake up, the church is empty except for them. When they open the doors to the church, they find themselves in a scene from Revelation. What is your reaction to this depiction of the end times? Is this the way you envision it?

- What effect did watching "Simpsons Bible Stories" have on the way you view the Bible? Did it change your mind in any way?

- After watching "Simpsons Bible Stories," do you feel that the Bible should be used as a foundation for humor?

- Do you think others might be encouraged to take a look at the Bible in response to watching "Simpsons Bible Stories?"

Prayer: God our Creator, the Bible is one of the most important foundations of our faith. Show us new ways to encounter your word and use it in our daily walk of faith. As we read the Scripture, help us to see your spirit moving so we can learn your will for our lives. Amen.

Something to Talk About: Find time this week to talk to someone you respect about the influence of the Bible in his or her life. What part does the Bible play in this person's life on a daily basis? At what time was the Bible most important to him or her?

Nine

Calling and Tradition

Episode: "Like Father, Like Clown"
(*The Best of* The Simpsons, vol. 11)

Synopsis: When Krusty the Clown comes over for dinner, the Simpsons learn that he is Jewish. As Krusty shares his life story, we learn that he is the son of a rabbi who wanted his son to follow in his footsteps. Krusty, however, felt called to become a clown and entertain people. When Krusty defied his father in order to pursue his calling, his father disowned him. Bart and Lisa make it their mission to reconcile father and son.

Supplementary Reading: Chapter 10 of *The Gospel according to* The Simpsons

Old Testament Scripture Lesson (Deut. 10:19): You shall also love the stranger, for you were strangers in the land of Egypt.
(Ps. 69:8): I have become a stranger to my kindred, an alien to my mother's children.

New Testament Scripture Lesson (1 Cor. 12:4–7): Now there are varieties of gifts, but the same Spirit; and there are varieties of services, but the same Lord; and there are varieties of activities, but it is the same God who activates all of them in everyone. To each is given the manifestation of the Spirit for the common good.

Questions for Discussion: Prior to the discussion, have a member of the group read each of the Scripture lessons.

- How do the Simpsons find out that Krusty is Jewish? (When asked to say grace, he prays in Hebrew.)

- How does Homer react to Krusty's prayer? (Homer laughs because he thinks Krusty is making up a gibberish language, but Lisa sets him straight.)

- How does Homer react to the revelation that Krusty is Jewish? (Homer is shocked. It's almost as if he's never met a Jew before.)

- What does Krusty's father do for a living? (Krusty's father is a rabbi, a spiritual leader of the Jewish people.)

- Krusty tells the Simpsons the story of his childhood, including the first time he asked his father, "When I grow up can I be a clown?" How did his father react? (His father is vehemently opposed to the idea. He says, "A clown is not a respected member of the community.")

- When Krusty says to his father, "I want to make people laugh," how does his father reply? (Krusty's father says, "Life is not fun; life is serious.")

- Krusty says, "Dad wanted me to follow in his footsteps, but the pull of clowning was too strong." What is Krusty describing here? (Krusty is describing his calling. He does not feel called to be a rabbi; instead, he feels called to be a clown. All he really wants is for his calling to be affirmed and accepted by his father.)

- Read 1 Corinthians 12:4–7 again. What does this verse have to say about spiritual gifts and calling?

- Could Krusty have been a good rabbi? (Krusty's father says that Krusty was first in his yeshiva class [a yeshiva is an orthodox Jewish rabbinical seminary] and that he was voted "most likely to hear God." He probably could have been a good rabbi, but was not feeling called in that direction, so his heart would have never been completely in it.)

- When Krusty's father discovers that he has become a clown in spite of his wishes, how does he react? (He says, "You have brought shame on our family," and disowns him.)

• Have you felt a sense of calling? If you have, do the people you love support you in that calling?

• How does Krusty react to being rejected by his father? (He is depressed. He cries when he sees a copy of *Modern Jewish Father* magazine. He calls his father on the phone but is unable to speak. He speaks fondly about the father and son relationships in an *Itchy and Scratchy* cartoon.)

• Why doesn't Krusty want to leave the Simpsons' house after dinner? (Krusty doesn't want to leave the Simpsons' house because he enjoys feeling like part of a family.)

• What do Bart and Lisa decide to do? (Lisa says, "A man who envies our family is a man who needs help." They decide to find a way to reconcile Krusty and his father.)

• Bart calls in to the radio show to ask, "If a son defies his father and chooses a career that makes millions of children happy, shouldn't the father forgive the son?" Why is Krusty's father so quick to answer this question "No"? (He feels that Krusty has turned his back on their tradition, their faith, and him.)

• What is tradition? How is tradition a good thing? Is tradition always a good thing? (Tradition is the handing down of values, beliefs, and customs from one generation to the next. It is a way of doing things and seeing the world that has helped sustain a community in the past.)

• How do Bart and Lisa decide to convince Krusty's father to forgive him? (Lisa determines that the one thing rabbis value the most is knowledge, so she and Bart research Jewish thought to find knowledge that will convince Krusty's father to give Krusty a second chance.)

• The first quote Lisa uncovers is, "A child should be pushed aside with the left hand and drawn closer with the right. What do you think this means? (One way of interpreting this saying would be that parents need to prepare for and accept their children's independence, but continue loving them no matter what happens.)

- What finally convinces Krusty's father to forgive him? (Bart quotes from *Yes, I Can* by Sammy Davis Jr., a Jewish entertainer. Krusty's father laments his inability to see the value in Krusty's calling.)

> "The Jews are a swinging bunch of people. I mean, I've heard of persecution, but what they went through is ridiculous. But the great thing is after thousands of years of waiting and holding on and fighting they finally made it." Quoted by Bart from *Yes, I Can* by Sammy Davis Jr.

- Read the story of the Prodigal Son (Luke 15:11–32). What aspects of this story apply to the relationship between Krusty and his father?

You can use the quote above to facilitate a discussion about Judaism and the way the Jews have been treated throughout history. Some questions you might ask could include:

- What does this episode of *The Simpsons* have to say about the Jews and being Jewish?

- Are you aware of the history of the persecution of the Jews?

- Do you realize that many of the earliest Christians still considered themselves Jewish?

- Can you imagine what it is like to be a religious minority?

- Do you think of America as a "Christian nation?"

- What does it mean to us as Americans to have freedom of religion?

- Should a minority ever have to change its worldview to reflect the majority opinion?

- Are you aware that Christians are a persecuted minority in some parts of the world?

- How do you think your life would change if you were a member of a persecuted minority?

- Have you ever been invited to a synagogue or a temple, perhaps to attend a bar mitzvah or bat mitzvah?

- The first time you visited, did you find it strange?

- How was it different from the church services you are more familiar with?

- Have you ever spent time in the home of a Jewish friend? A Muslim or Hindu friend? Was it different? Were you made to feel comfortable?

- Do you think that is how members of other faiths feel in this country?

Prayer: Our Heavenly Creator, guide us as we seek to find a sense of calling in our lives. No matter what we do with our lives, we want you to be an important part of them. Help those who love us to support us in our calling. Whatever we are called to do, let it be for you. Amen.

Something to Talk About: Find time this week to talk to someone you respect about calling. Did this person feel called to do what he or she is doing in life? What part does this person's faith play in his or her sense of calling? OR—Talk to a Jewish friend about his or her faith. How is it different from your faith? How is it similar?

Ten

Knowing God and Being Part
of a Community of Faith

Episode: "Homer the Heretic"
(At present this episode is commercially unavailable. Check with your
Fox television affiliate for broadcast times so you can watch it as a group.)

Synopsis: While getting ready for church, Homer splits his
pants and decides not to attend. The furnace at the church is
broken, so the family suffers through the service while Homer has
a great time at home. Homer has such a good time that he decides
to stop attending church altogether. Homer then has a dream in
which God appears to him. At first God is angry with Homer for
abandoning the church, but then God agrees to allow Homer to
worship him in his own way. Homer dons a monk's robe and
decides to create his own religion. When Homer falls asleep while
smoking a cigar, the house catches on fire. His friends and neighbors on the volunteer fire department extinguish the blaze. Saved
from the disaster, Homer agrees to give church another try and is
soon snoring away in the front pew.

Supplementary Reading: Chapter 1 of *The Gospel according to
The Simpsons*

Old Testament Scripture Lesson (Exod. 34:5–8): The LORD
descended in the cloud and stood with him there, and proclaimed
the name, "The LORD." The LORD passed before him, and proclaimed, "The LORD, the LORD, a God merciful and gracious, slow
to anger, and abounding in steadfast love and faithfulness, keeping
steadfast love for the thousandth generation, forgiving iniquity and

transgression and sin, yet by no means clearing the guilty, but visiting the iniquity of the parents upon the children and the children's children, to the third and the fourth generation." And Moses quickly bowed his head toward the earth, and worshiped.

New Testament Scripture Lesson (Acts 17:23–27): [Paul said to the Athenians,] "For as I went through the city and looked carefully at the objects of your worship, I found among them an altar with the inscription, 'To an unknown god.' What therefore you worship as unknown, this I proclaim to you. The God who made the world and everything in it, he who is Lord of heaven and earth, does not live in shrines made by human hands, nor is he served by human hands, as though he needed anything, since he himself gives to all mortals life and breath and all things. From one ancestor he made all nations to inhabit the whole earth, and he allotted the times of their existence and the boundaries of the places where they would live, so that they would search for God and perhaps grope for him and find him—though indeed he is not far from each one of us.

Questions for Discussion: Prior to the discussion, have a member of the group read aloud each of the Scripture lessons.

• At the beginning of the episode, Marge is trying to get Homer out of bed so he can attend worship services. She says, "It's church, you have to go!" Do you feel like going to church is a duty?

• When Marge gets home she asks Homer, "Are you actually giving up your faith?" At first Homer answers no and then changes to yes. Is being part of a church community and attending worship services a necessary aspect of faith?

• In his defense Homer asks, "What's the big deal about going to some building every Sunday? Isn't God everywhere?" How would you respond to him?

• Homer also argues, "Don't you think the Almighty has better things to worry about than where one little guy spends one measly hour of his week?" How would you respond to this?

- Homer then says, "What if we picked the wrong religion? Every week we're just making God madder and madder." Do you think there is such a thing as a "wrong religion?" If so, what makes a religion wrong or right?

- How do you feel about Homer suggesting that God responds to us out of anger? Is this a fair characterization of God?

- Bart enters the debate on his father's side, and it's clear that Homer's witness is affecting Bart's values. How important do you think it is for parents to attend worship services as an example to their children?

- Do you think Homer realizes the effect his witness has on Bart?

- God appears to Homer in a dream. How do you feel about God making a personal appearance in Homer's life?

- Can you name some times in the Bible when God communicated with human beings through dreams? (Two examples would include Solomon [1 Kings 3:5] and Joseph, Jesus' father [Matthew 1:20])

- Read Exodus 34:5–8 again. What is the difference between God appearing to Moses and God appearing to Homer? (Moses is a great leader and Homer is just an average guy. Moses has been called to carry God's law to the people of Israel and Homer has simply decided not to attend church. Both of them, however, are able to have a personal conversation with God.)

- What do we learn about God based on his appearance to Moses? (God is "merciful," "gracious" and "slow to anger," "keeping steadfast love for the thousandth generation." However, God will deal severely with those who are guilty.)

- Based on his appearance to Homer, what is God like? (Initially God is angry with Homer, but God listens to what Homer has to say and is reasonable. He obviously cares for Homer personally. God is willing to give Homer's new way of looking at the world a chance.)

- God's opening words to Homer are an angry, "Thou hast forsaken my church!" Do you think failing to attend worship services is the same thing as forsaking God?

- Homer argues, "I'm not a bad guy. I work hard. I love my kids. Why should I spend half my Sunday hearing how I'm going to hell?" God's response is, "You've got a point there." Does Homer have a point?

- Homer tells God, "You know what I really hate about church? Those boring sermons." Do we have a right to expect a certain quality of sermon and worship experience? Should a "boring sermon" be a reason not to attend church?

- God agrees with Homer about the boring sermons and tells Homer that Reverend Lovejoy displeases him. In fact, God says he is going to give Reverend Lovejoy a canker sore. Do you think God is involved in determining the events of our lives to this level of detail?

- Homer tells God, "I figure I should try to live right and worship you in my own way." How do you feel about this argument?

- What advantages does being part of a worshiping community give us? (Obviously there are many good reasons to be part of a worshiping community. Two of the most important are for the support we receive from others in our spiritual walk and the fact that worshiping with others calls us into accountability for the way we live our lives.)

- Why do you think God gives Homer the option to worship in "his own way?" (One reason might be that God wants Homer to discover the importance of his community of faith on his own.)

- When Lisa asks Homer, "Why are you dedicating your life to blasphemy?" Homer replies, "Don't worry sweetheart, if I'm wrong I'll recant on my deathbed." How do you feel about this philosophy? Are "deathbed" confessions fair?

• How does Marge deal with Homer's decision? (Marge is an excellent witness. She keeps on attending church. She prays about the situation and for Homer in particular. She reminds Homer of their responsibility to raise the children right. She puts God first and even gives Homer an ultimatum: "Don't make me choose between my man and my God because you just can't win.")

• When the house catches on fire Lisa says, "Truly this is an act of God." Do you agree with her?

• When Homer is asked what he learned he replies, "God is vengeful." Is Homer being fair with God?

• How do the others respond to Homer's characterization of God as vengeful? (Ned Flanders tells Homer, "God didn't set your house on fire." Reverend Lovejoy says, "He was working in the hearts of your friends and neighbors when they went to your aid.")

• Why do you think Homer decides to give church another try?

• The episode ends with Homer falling asleep in church and dreaming that he is walking and talking with God. Do you wish you could have that kind of direct relationship with God?

• How do you know that God is a part of your life?

• Read Acts 17:23–27 again. How does Paul suggest that we can know God without having the kind of experience that Homer has?

Prayer: Our heavenly Creator, we seek to feel the power of your presence and to know you more completely. While you may not appear to us in our dreams, we know your spirit is real as we sense it moving in the world around us. Help us to reflect your love into the world and to see your spirit in others. Amen.

Something to Talk About: Find time this week to talk to some-one you respect about how he or she views God. Has this person ever had an experience that he or she would consider a divine rev-elation? OR—Talk to somebody you respect about how being part of a community of faith plays an important role in his or her life.

.